Concert and Contest COLLECTION

Compiled and Edited by H. VOXMAN

for

E♭ or BB♭ BASS (Tuba-Sousaphone) with piano accompaniment

CONTENTS

RUBANK®

HAL•LEONARD® CORPORATION
7777 W. BLUEMOUND RD. P.O. BOX 13819 MILWAUKEE, WI 53213

Sarabanda and Gavotta

A. CORELLI
Transcribed by H. Voxman

Allegro moderato

Waltz and Galop
from Petite Suite

D. KABALEVSKY
Transcribed by H. Voxman

Allegro

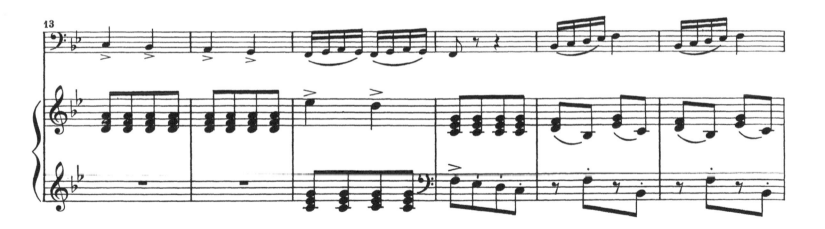

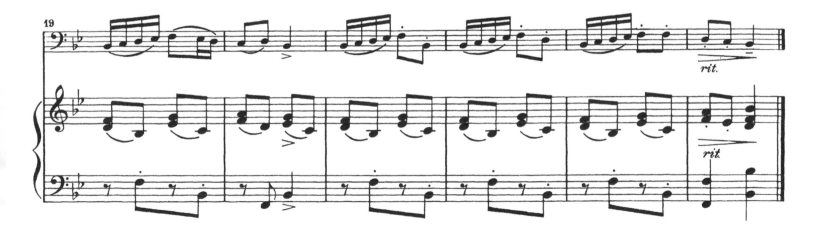

Two Short Pieces

G. F. HANDEL
Transcribed by H. Voxman

ARIA (Rinaldo)

BOURRÉE

Allegro [♩ = 72]

Premier Solo de Concours

RENÉ MANIET
Transcribed by H. Voxman

10

Largo and Allegro

Continuo realized
by R. Hervig

B. MARCELLO
Transcribed by H. Voxman

Air Gai

G. P. BERLIOZ
Transcribed by H. Voxman

Andante and Allegro

ROBERT CLÉRISSE
Transcribed by H. Voxman

Andante Cantabile
from Concerto

N. RIMSKY-KORSAKOV
Transcribed by H. Voxman

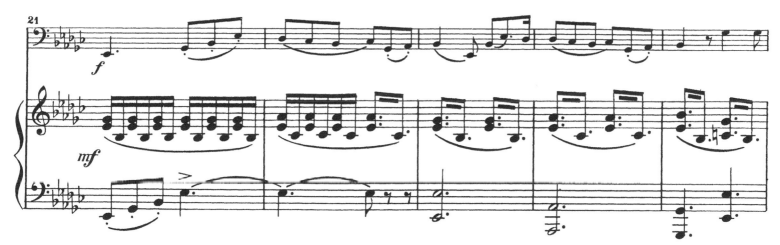

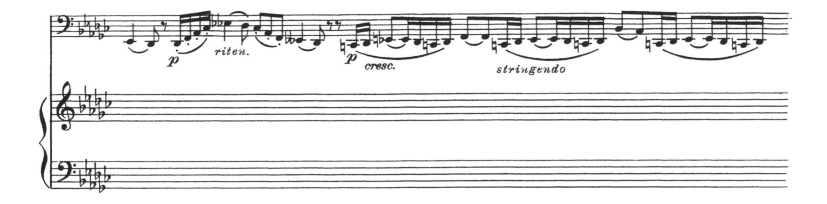

Persiflage

PAUL KOEPKE

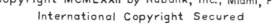

28

Adagio and Allegro
from Sonata No. 7

Continuo realized
by R. Hervig

G. F. HANDEL
Transcribed by H. Voxman

First Movement
from Concerto for Horn

W. A. MOZART
Transcribed by H. Voxman

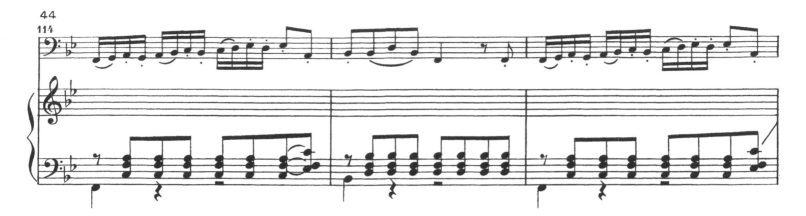

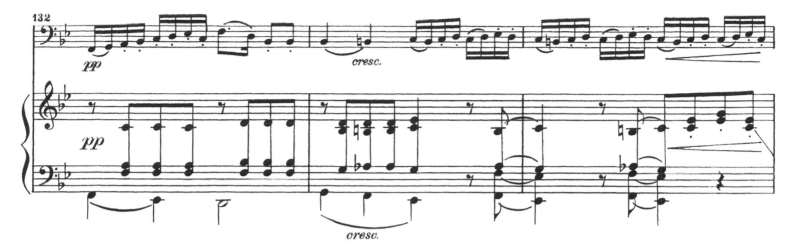

Serenade and Scherzo

LEROY OSTRANSKY

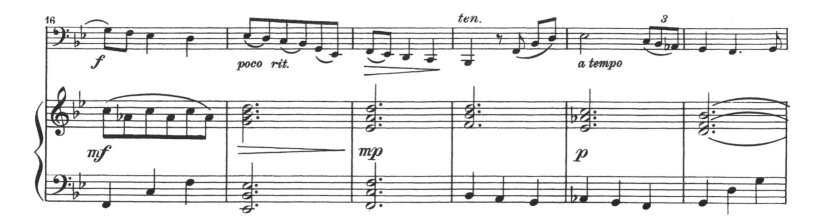

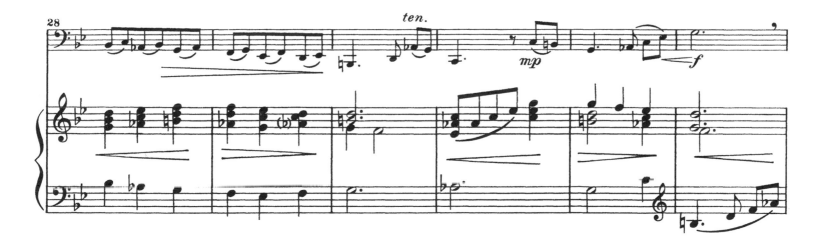

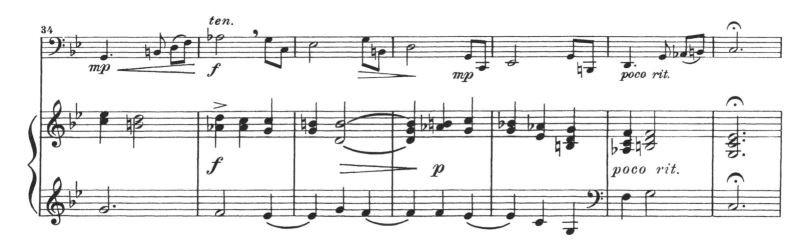

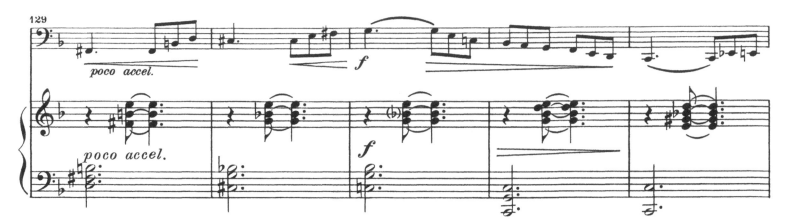

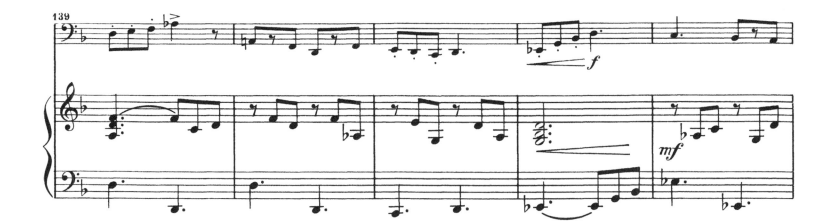

Morceau de Concours

G. ALARY, Op. 57
Transcribed by H. Voxman

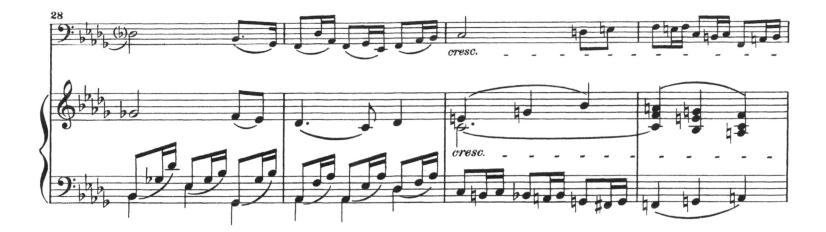

Allegro energico (♪=♩)

Adagio and Finale
from Concertino

CHARLES GAUCET
Transcribed by H. Voxman

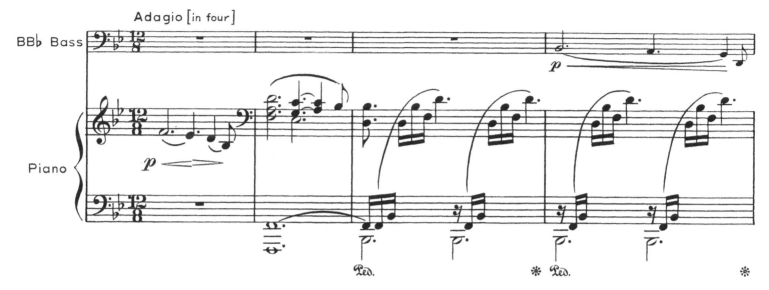

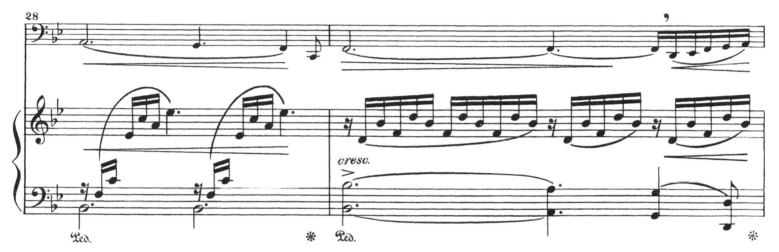

FINALE
Allegro moderato